Eat Well
Stay Fit

Eat Well Stay Fit

DIE ANYWAY

AND MORE

Holy Moly!

RULES OF MODERN LIFE

FRIDAY BOOKS

First published in Great Britain in 2006 by Friday Books
An imprint of The Friday Project Limited
83 Victoria Street, London SW1H 0HW

www.thefridayproject.co.uk
www.fridaybooks.co.uk

ISBN 10 – 1 905548 29 X
ISBN 13 – 978 1 905548 29 3

British Library Cataloguing in Publication Data

A catalogue record for this book is available
from the British Library

1 3 5 7 9 10 8 6 4 2

Designed by Paul Ashby

Produced by Staziker Jones
www.stazikerjones.co.uk

The Publisher's policy is to use paper
manufactured from sustainable forests.

Introduction

Hello

It appears that not enough people took notice of the last book. There are still blue Subarus filled with men wearing trainers with no socks on the roads, Tia Maria is still for sale and people still insist on having pointless dogs (clue: if you can pick it up – it isn't any use).

Such is the ferocity of Holy Moly readers, I've managed to gather together another feast of anger-venting, life-affirming spite. Good on you moles.

For as long as there is lettuce in salads (Go on, try describing its taste.) and *Little Miss Jocelyn* on the television, there is a need for you. Stick a finger up the arse of celebrity and stupidity and be proud of it.

Love, Mr Holy Moly

1

You can have your cake and eat it by simply purchasing two.

2 Take your time young man.
Don't you rush to get old.

3 In an argument about any subject at all,
the first person to refer to George Orwell
or to make a comparison with Nazi
Germany has automatically lost.

4 Anything that comes in a tin cannot by
itself be called a meal.

5 While on stage, Bono could not be further from The Edge even if he tried.

6 **Gays!**
Calling a man 'she' is not hilarious in itself.

7 Taking a shit at school is probably the hardest thing a kid will have to go through.

8 Never wear boxers without washing them first otherwise you're likely to end up with a fluffy bell-end.

9

The collective term for a group of slags is a 'limousine'.

10

Goth girls!
Going to Halloween parties dressed as that scary woman in *The Ring* is hardly pushing the boat out.

11 If you like her, you'll fuck it up.

12 Never moon at a werewolf.

13

Gypsies!
Avoid hassle from the authorities and eventual eviction from your illegal site by putting up a few fairground rides.

14
If you can afford to smoke, you can afford mouthwash and toothpaste: try using them, you stank-mouthed cunt.

15
People!
If you are walking down a busy street do not assume that I will always be on the look out for you and your immovable shoulders of steel.

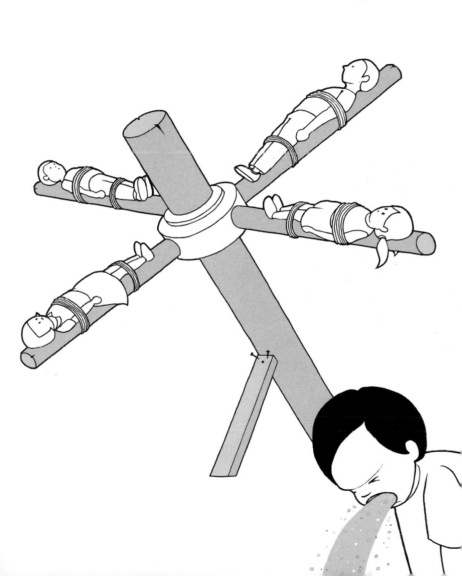

16

Thai fisherman's pants should never, repeat NEVER, be worn in a city. Unless, of course, you are in fact a Thai fisherman attending an international symposium on fishing wear.

17 When in a pub it is acceptable practice to applaud if someone drops a glass. It is not acceptable practice however, to applaud if someone gets glassed.

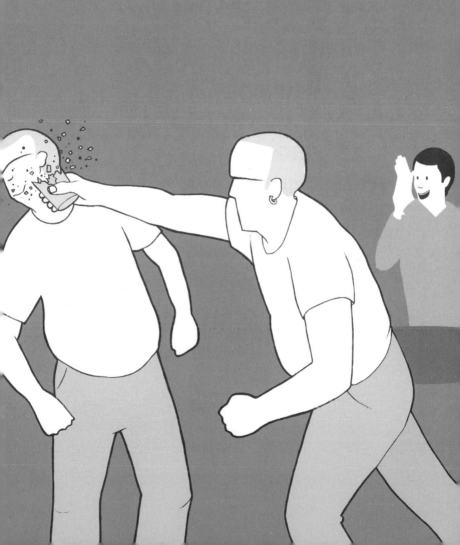

18

Sandwich Shop Workers!

After serving customers, please allow at least 10 seconds between them placing their sandwich and yoghurt crunch thing on the counter and you asking them for £160.77. They will need a few seconds to absorb the mind-numbing shock that this is indeed the price of their lunch and they are not being mugged.

19 The university of life has no entry requirements and just as many smug useless cunts as the University of Durham.

20 Bland thin actresses with negligible talent! Hook up with a pretty actor and always wear floppy hats and overpriced 'ethnic' necklaces. That way you'll be described as 'boho' and 'edgy' thus disguising the fact you're just a dull, blonde, thin actress with Dairylea for brains.

21 **Women driving Nissan Micras!** Half a toy shop of cuddly toys in your back window does not hide the fact that you are still driving a Micra.

When in the front of the queue at the lights try putting it in gear BEFORE the lights go green, not fucking 15 minutes after they have gone green for the seventh time.

22 **Changing your name doesn't make you cooler, it makes you cuntier!**
Take note Jude – should that be DAVE – Law.

23 **Lounge Lizards!**
Wearing shoes without socks in winter does not make you look interesting and Mediterranean. It makes you look like a cold-ankled wanker.

24 **Smoking IS cool!**
It may not be clever, but it IS cool.

Plastering is NOT an art-form.

Men!

26 Once you leave college/university/get your first job, bin your skateboard, rollerblades, knee and elbow pads. DON'T trade them in for two wheels, a day-glo lycra body condom, crash hat and fake Oakleys. Grow up, get a licence and go about in an adult manner.

27 **Music shop assistants!** Don't berate my purchases to other staff until I've left.

28 Dont confuse Greeks with Geeks: one invented homosexuality, the others are geeks.

Eat well,
Stay fit,
Die anyway.

29

30

Strangers are not friends
waiting to happen...

Strangers are rape in a dark
alley waiting to happen.

31 If it's a big round, order the Guinness first. Barmen, if it's a big round, pour the Guinness first...

32 **Staff at trendy bars!**
While you work in the bar you can drop the attitude. I care not that you may 'actually' be a writer/actor/photographer/DJ. In the bar you are 'actually' bar staff and you can be easily replaced by Eastern Europeans who have better attitudes and who in reality are probably better writer/actor/photographer/DJs than you.

33 If in doubt, don't think W.W.J.C.D think W.W.J.L.D (What Would John Leslie Do) and this should sort any moral dilemmas out nicely.

34

Never perform a 'dance-off' once you're aged 12+.

35 Never trust a man calling himself
a film-maker.
Pete Doherty will back me up here.

36 'Angels' by Robbie Williams will win
ANY musical poll decided by the public.
Ditto *The Da Vinci Code* with books.

37 If you're British, never say
'You do the math'.

39

Jamiroquai fans!
Save money by not buying the 'new' Jamiroquai album, realising instead that it's the same turgid, derivative toss as the previous Jamiroquai album, and all Jamiroquai albums before that.
(See also Metallica).

People who make boxer shorts!
Stop with the fiddly hole for your knob to
go through. Any fucker who's too lazy
to pull the front down while taking a piss
deserves to face the consequences.

Only paedos wear Speedos.

Music from 20 years ago is brilliant.
Music from 10 years ago is shit.
Regardless of what year it is this rule will
always apply. The only exception to the
rule is Razorlight, who will always be shit.

When in Rome – visit the Colosseum.

 If you've ever said:
'I don't drink/do drugs, I'm crazy enough as I am, can you imagine what I'd be like if I drank/did drugs?' – kill yourself.

 Never trust vending machines. They have a habit of giving you Lemon Lilt instead of Fanta Orange.

 Everyone loves the smell of their own poo.

Never bet on a dog named Tripod.

Never play leapfrog with a Unicorn.

 **Not all roads lead to Rome...
the M25 for example.**

 Music video by music video, Beyoncé is slowly morphing into Tina Turner. Any day now Jay-z is going to beat the fuck out of her.

Always check everyone else is skinny dipping before you do...

52 Every bloke has at some stage while taking a pee, flushed halfway through and then raced against the flush.

53 If you want a varied positional sex life, don't build an Ikea loft bed in a low-ceilinged room. It smacks of pessimism.

54 When required to do an impression of a cow, don't just say moo. Do an impression of someone from Northern Ireland saying 'mirror'.

55

If you look a gift horse in the mouth you're unlikely to notice it shitting on your carpet.

56

The collective noun for a group of leery young men in gaudy shirts is a 'Stella'.

57 Always staple things. It generates a feeling of achievement and organisation, and makes you feel good.

58 Gold is worth its weight in gold.

59 Every man has a friend called Big Al or Big Dave.

60 It is impossible to do a Fred Elliott impression without saying 'I say, I say... '

61 If you are gay and can say a sexual innuendo, you will get your own talk show.

62 The posher the name of the cigarette the poorer the smoker: Mayfair, Sovereign, Richmond, Royals.

63 Everyone owns a Nokia charger.

64

Girls who drive sports cars very rarely enjoy sex and still call their parents Mummy and Daddy.

65

Aqua is not an ingredient, it is a colour. Stop putting it on everything to try and disguise the fact that the product that costs twenty quid is actually ninety fucking per cent water.

66 **Advertisers!**
The play on the words 'organic' and 'orgasmic' is not and never has been funny. Stop it now.

67 The hum you hear when an electric car goes by is not the vehicle's motor, but in fact the hum of the driver's self-righteousness oscillating at a high frequency.

68 The time it takes for a DVD player to eject a DVD is inversely proportional to the time it takes the person you live with to walk from the front door into the room where you are.

69 It is impossible to watch *The Champ* and not cry.

70

Only ugly women are 'on-line now' on any dating site'.

71 If you're bored, try asking women of your acquaintance to attempt to make machine gun noises.

72 If you have a wank in the bath, always make sure you've got a comb handy.

73 The youngest person you can go out with = half your age + 7.

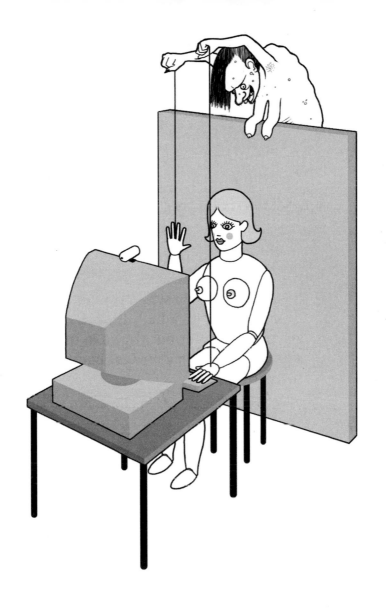

74 Flashing your car headlights can mean 'After you', 'Look Out', 'You're an Idiot', 'Thank You', 'I fancy you', 'Hello, Mate', 'You're going too fast', 'You're going too slow', 'There's a speed trap 100 yards up the road', 'There's a serious malfunction with your automobile', 'Your headlights aren't on', or 'Your headlights are too bright'. It's all a matter of interpretation.

75 You can't eat trifle with a straw.

76 If your bed is cold when you get in, don't ever curl up into a ball. Granted, you will warm up quicker but you're in for a shock when you stretch your feet back down to the bottom.

77

The reason men fall asleep after ejaculation is the thought of having to do some sort of cleaning up.

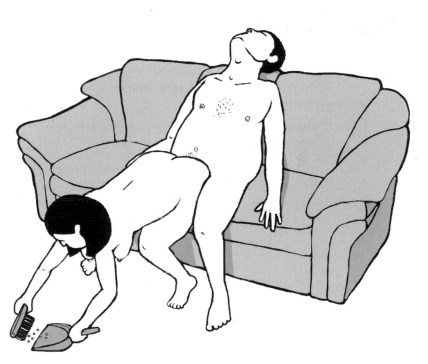

78

Don't pick John Prescott as a 'Happy Slap' target.

79 Goths are the most boring people on the planet. My arse has more inner darkness.

80 Never look directly at Zandra Rhodes.

81 If you say no to drugs, they won't listen.

82 J. Lo Glow and Chanel No. 5 wearers! Just remember what is actually contained within that £40 bottle. Within every perfume is a fixative. This is called ambergris, which is made from the indigestible parts of giant squid (particularly the beaks) and is found in the stomachs of blue whales. So, if you like wearing whale bile, spray away...

83 If you can make a spit string nearly reach the floor before you suck it back up, you are clearly destined for greatness!

84 Do not listen to the world – you will never understand.

85 Dogs chase cats, it is rarely the other way round. Unless you own a lion.

86 Always hold your breath and speed up your pace while walking through department store perfume and make-up areas. Otherwise you will vomit in front of an orange-faced cow trying to sell you something overpriced and pointless.

87 If you trip up or stumble in the street, always remember to look back and angrily glare at nothing at all on the pavement before squaring your shoulders, walking off and muttering 'Fucking cunt!'. It never fails to totally replenish your composure and ego, and wins the respect of passers-by.

88 Never trust a man with two mobiles.

89 People who say 'it's the luck of the draw' usually did better in the draw than you.

90

Ginger people!
Sitting in the front row of
a comedy club will cause
you to appear as if you are
holding a sign that says:
'Run out of material?
Dying? Don't worry, I'm
here, please have a go'.

Sexually repressed men!
When you next consider saying a girl
'looks like she's really filthy', be more
honest: 'I hope she sticks her thumb up
my arse' is always what you mean.

Ruby!
Don't take your love to town.

Mobile phones!
When my battery is low, don't warn me
every five minutes with more noise and
lights than ever considered possible. Now
I've got no battery what-so-fucking-ever.

Hairdressing salons always employ at least one of the following:

- a skinny gay man who, although his accent shouts Home Counties, is named Dieter or Sascha.

- a fat bird who dresses in a black tarpaulin, has purple eyeliner and smokes a lot.

- an old tart with cropped, bleached, spiky hair with more (silver) earrings than brain cells.

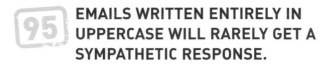

95 EMAILS WRITTEN ENTIRELY IN UPPERCASE WILL RARELY GET A SYMPATHETIC RESPONSE.

96 If at first you don't succeed, pay someone else to do it.

97 Over-friendly and drunk Glaswegians in smoky station bars, the effect when you hold my arm in a vice-like grip until my fingers turn blue as you say 'Now yu teek care o' ye sel' through your Grouse-soaked teeth, is less heart-warming and friendly than unpleasant and intimidating.

98 No news is Fox news.

99

The very last thing that a person who types ROTFLMAO will be doing is rolling on the floor laughing their ass off.

After buying a pot of cotton buds: immediately open it and knock or kick them to the floor, spilling them, then spend an infuriating five minutes trying to cram them back into the now shrunken pot. This is an inevitable sequence of events. Just get it over with.

101

People who don't vote in parliamentary elections but do vote for *Big Brother* evictions have absolutely no right to express their opinions about the actions of the Government.

102

Pissing on someone if they're on fire does not work, mainly because of stage fright.

103

Show me a man with pride and I'll show you a man with limited options.

104 There are only 10 types of people in the world. Those who understand binary and those who don't.

105 When going into a bookshop to buy a book on self-help, do not ask the lady behind the counter for assistance to find it as this defeats the object.

106 Money, keys, phone.

107 If you somehow managed to reanimate The Mamas and Papas, and got them to play covers of Kings of Leon songs, they would be The Magic Numbers.

Way to solve two of the world's biggest problems... feed the homeless to the hungry.

R'n'B stands for Rhythm and Blues: Muddy Waters, John Lee Hooker etc. Liberty X, Christina Milian and Black Eyed Peas do not do R'n'B, they do anodyne soul-destroying pop. Stop ruining the genre, you corporate whores.

110 If it's got wheels or tits it's going to cost a fortune.

111
Girls!
If you get a text from your boyfriend saying that he wants to kick your puppy and dual your aunt, take it with a pinch of salt as it's more likely that he just hasn't got the hang of predictive text yet...

112
Advertising Agencies!
85% Confusion, 15% Commission

113 Never wankthribble the cockpoop twatpenis; instead, shitfondling the arsedick will bring wankpiddling shitfucks.

114

The loudest, most boisterous muscle mary in the gym will always be the man who pulls his underpants up under his towel.

115

Time is a great healer, unless you're HIV positive.

116

There is no friendship, no love, like that of the parent for the child. Unless you're Fred and Rose West.

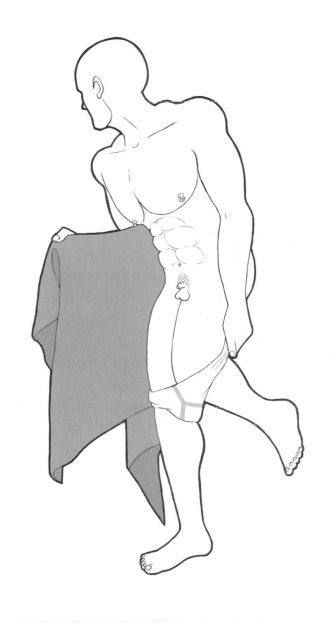

117

Drug-addled kids!
When choosing a car to break into, try and find one that looks like it might have something worth nicking inside rather than a manky, dust-encrusted car with only 20 cassettes, a road map and some travel rugs in. These are not worth a lot on the black market. Oh, and you won't find the Crown Jewels in the ashtray, despite looking there.

118 Unless you own a rap empire, please leave the chunky gold and 'ice' in the window of H. Samuel, where it can live a long and happy life doing nobody any harm.

119 Lie, steal, cheat.

120 Never raise your hands to your kids, it leaves your groin unprotected.

121

People who live in glass houses shouldn't masturbate with the lights on.

122

British spies!
Instead of spending thousands on a fake rock and hi-tech storage device why don't you just get a mobile like everyone else? You can get them from Tesco for about 20 quid.

123

Treat lesbians with the respect they deserve, after all they make really excellent films.

124 Always let the sun set on an argument. Assuming that no one actually dies in the night and leaves the other with a lifetime of guilt, the issue will inevitably seem much less worth screaming over after a good night's sleep.

125 Newsagents will not sell out of all their papers by 7am. It is therefore unnecessary for pensioners to be at the shop as they open their doors.

You'll never see a pregnant Goth.

127

If you can keep your head when all around you are losing theirs, you obviously don't understand the severity of the situation.

128 It's 'eT cetera', not 'eX cetera', you damp-assed, armpit-farting 'eXpresso' drinker.

129 Referring to yourself in the third person is an excellent method of demonstrating what a complete dick you are. Holy Moly! doesn't like it.

What minimal credibility is granted by having gone to Glastonbury is immediately negated by drunkenly admitting you 'knew the Beautiful South would put on a solid show'.

131 Political correctness makes it difficult to be straight with a gay.

132 Putting a bit, then leaving...

...a bloody great gap does NOT make your joke any funnier.

133 Everyone who has been in a supermarket will have said at some time 'This trolley has a mind of its own' despite the fact it clearly has not. It's just the wheels are fucked.

134 Don't EVER sleep with your female friends. Even if you firmly agree that 'it is just sex', 'of course there won't be any comeback', 'this won't affect our friendship' and 'I don't expect anything from you', you can damn well guarantee that, upon not taking the second phone call of the last five minutes, said female friend will turn into a wailing harpie demanding that 'we meet to sort things out' and subsequently accuse you of ignoring her, being evasive, treating her like a whore, blah, blah fucking blah. Alternatively, do turn up at the meeting, admit that you are a cunt and keep that particular 'door' ajar just enough.

135 Tom Cruise is fucked.

136 Jimmy Carr is annoying.

e = mc hammer.

138

Two heads aren't necessarily better than one. Have you ever seen a conjoined twin smiling?

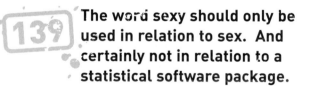

139 The word sexy should only be used in relation to sex. And certainly not in relation to a statistical software package.

140 People who don't drink cannot be trusted.

141 **Americans!**
Keep using the word 'fanny' as a slang term for your bottom. It's hilarious.

142 iPod = iCunt

143 30-something men that work in IT for London firms should refrain from thinking of themselves as extreme sports hellmen. So you've been snowboarding twice and rented a surfboard for two hours in Newquay when you were 11. This does not give you a licence to refer to things as 'rad', 'sick' or 'gnarly'. You sound like a cunt.

144 People with speech impediments should only be allowed to speak for a few hours a day. They become quite annoying after a while.

The lower the income,
the greater the number
of Sky TV channels
subscribed to.

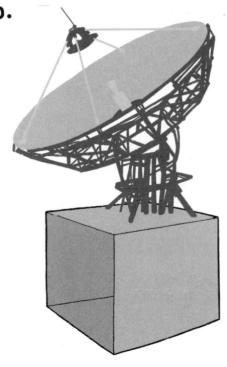

146

Gypsies!

Learn how to paint fake Disney characters on your fairground rides better. Donald Duck is unlikely to endear children if he looks like he has a hernia.

If you own a scooter and are not in advertising, you are a wanker. If you are in advertising, you are a wanker with or without a scooter.

Women will buy anything if they think it makes them look younger. Men will buy anything if they think it will get them laid.

Writing a book about the fact that you have just purchased an electronic music device, which every other tool on the planet has had for about three years, is guaranteed only to elicit derisory laughter, even from your old 'mates' on GQ.

Students!

The more people who are likely to be endangered/inadvertently killed, the better the sign you have stolen.

151

Drunken people being arrested on fly-on-the-wall programmes about the police! Always remember to be violent and abusive towards the arresting officers whilst protesting your innocence. It'll be the crucial factor in getting released immediately.

152
I turned around and said... and then he
turned around and said... No, no, no.
Neither of you moved, I was watching.
You did, however, look a bit of a twat.

153
When ordering a coffee in the UK, use the
following structure: 'Please may I have
xxxx'. Under no circumstances should you
say 'Can I get xxxx'. This makes you sound
like a pathetic, shallow, easily influenced
dickhead who relies on American sitcoms
for your means of communication.

154
Americans!
'Mathematics' is a plural word (note the
fucking 's'), therefore its contraction is also
plural and thus also requires an 's'.

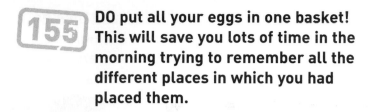

155 DO put all your eggs in one basket! This will save you lots of time in the morning trying to remember all the different places in which you had placed them.

156 *Mona Lisa Smile* is only worth watching if you're deaf and want a good wank.

157

The real trouble with reality is
that there's no background music.

158 Never let the truth stand in the way of a good rumour.

159 If you walk out of a pub and down the street with a half-drunk pint in your hand you will feel a bit harder than usual but also slightly nervous.

160

Homeless people!
Why sit next to cash machines? You're only winding yourselves up. You don't get blind people camping outside Specsavers or the deaf outside HMV... unless they are waiting in line for the Gareth Gates comeback album.

Mentally retarded dwarves are not big and they're not clever.

162

When the recently bereaved family of a murder victim hold a press conference, the one who blubs the most uncontrollably is probably the one who did it.

163 Elvis is dead, get over it.

164 Much like the members of The Beatles, Labour politicians will die in the wrong order.

165 **Public Sector Workers!**
The thin film of water that can appear on the brow of a person (not working in the public sector) is called sweat. It results from hard work.

166 **Magazine/newspaper people!**
If you use the headline 'Who's That Girl?' above a picture of a ropy-looking woman we *instantly* know it is Madonna looking a bit shit. You have been using this headline since the mid '80s, please think up something new so we can at least spend some time - oooh say about two seconds - giving a shit at guessing who that girl is. Thanks.

Smack is a great slimming aid. Failing that, cocaine is a sure-fire alternative.

**Street-based clipboard-
holding charity workers!**
As I walk towards you
desperately trying to avoid
making eye-contact, doing
a stupid little dance like a
jester in a cagoule does not
make me more likely to stop.

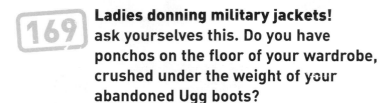

169 Ladies donning military jackets! ask yourselves this. Do you have ponchos on the floor of your wardrobe, crushed under the weight of your abandoned Ugg boots?

170 Too many cocks spoil the brothel.

171 It's almost impossible to sleep once you know there's a spider in your bedroom.

172 Pineapple juice smells like sick.

173 **Non-Londoners!**
The reason why 'nobody is talking to anyone else' on the tube is that we don't tend, unlike you, to talk to people we don't know.

174 Constantly repeating soundbites from hip new comedies within an office environment will not by default make you either hip or funny. It will simply accentuate what a friendless cunt you are. MY ARSE!

175

You can't outstare an owl – don't bother trying.

176 If you want to know what you'd look like as Pete Townsend of The Who simply look at your reflection in the back of a spoon.

177 You have to be 100% behind someone before you can stab them in the back.

Never put off what you can avoid all together.

 Encyclopaedias make very bad gifts for teenagers because they already know fucking everything.

 A rolling Moss gathers stoners.

Never kill a ladybird...
they have special powers.

There's no point wasting valuable seconds watching airline cabin crews demonstrate how to use a lifejacket. Planes don't 'land' on water, they crash into it at about 600 miles an hour and, at that point, you won't be in a fit state to work out how to get the straps over your head, tie them in a knot and work out how to blow the tiny plastic whistle. Just tune out and continue getting pissed.

Rock legends!

183 Whilst having an anecdote about killing your wife is pretty cool, you may well find it better if you do actually kill her before she turns you into some shitty house husband whilst she goes out and pretends to shop in Asda, whilst dragging your good name through the mud on the X-Factor.

184 Remember laughter's the best medicine, unless you're asthmatic, then it's Ventolin.

185 The less interesting the drug, the louder you will be when taking it.

186 Cheggers can't be boozers.

The longer the hair, the longer the guitar solo.

188 Any girls who dot their 'i's with hearts or circles get knocked up at least twice by the age of 16.

189 Space Raider crisps are the only product that have successfully avoided the effects of inflation.

190 Even the lesser-known tribes in darkest Botswana knew Kate Moss was a serial drug user.

191

You can go anywhere you want if you look serious and carry a clipboard.

192

If you're going to make a rape allegation against a footballer, don't go out on the town with him after the incident. It'll only make you look like a cheap prostitute.

193 The best bouncers/doorstaff manage to combine the intimidating bulk of a runaway combine harvester with the tact and diplomacy of a runaway combine harvester.

194 Home-fucking is killing prostitution.

195 No woman is ever truly happy until she can find a boyfriend who can make her miserable.

196 Whoever said 'nothing is impossible' has clearly never tried slamming a revolving door.

197 **Pikey mothers!**
Prevent your kids from getting murdered by keeping an eye on them occasionally.

198 Absence makes the heart grow fonder... of somebody else.

199 Phonetically speaking the alphabet to confirm your postcode will make you feel – if only for a second – like you are in the police or the army.
Bravo.

200 People who get stoned shouldn't throw glass houses.

201 You know it's time to kill yourself when you realise that both David Blunkett and Stephen Hawking have had more sex than you.

202

When killing someone by dropping an electrical appliance into their bathtub, be sure to disconnect the earth from the plug otherwise your circuit breaker will trip and you'll be doing an eight-year stretch for attempted murder.

203

It's a fine line between 'thinking out of the box' and 'talking out of your arse'.

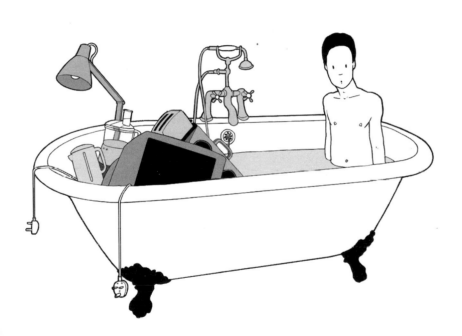

204 Car Dealers!
An inflatable zeppelin, no matter how attractive, is unlikely to drag me away from my daily tasks to spend £12,000 on a Citroën.

205
Pot noodles aren't sexy, bad, posh or sleazy. They are merely shit.

206 Assistants in 'trendy shops'!
You can stand there eyeing me up and looking aloof all you fucking want. I'm not the one jockeying a cash register nor do I need a staff discount to afford any of the items you're selling.

207

Frogs are fun ONLY in moderation.

Any man who says that
tongue piercings make
for a better blowjob is
both a liar and a weirdo.

209

It is a legal requirement when buying
a Vauxhall vehicle to have at least one
of the following:

a) A four-year-old England flag hanging
off the aerial.

b) A bulldog, either as a tattoo, a window
sticker or an animal.

c) A criminal record with shades of White
Supremacy leanings.

d) An ugly wife.

210 The more glamorous and exotic the name, the less convincing the tranny.

211 Although they won't admit it, Australians know they have no influence on world affairs.

212 Anybody who appears on *The Apprentice* probably has PC World, Pret a Manger or Dixons hidden somewhere on their CV.

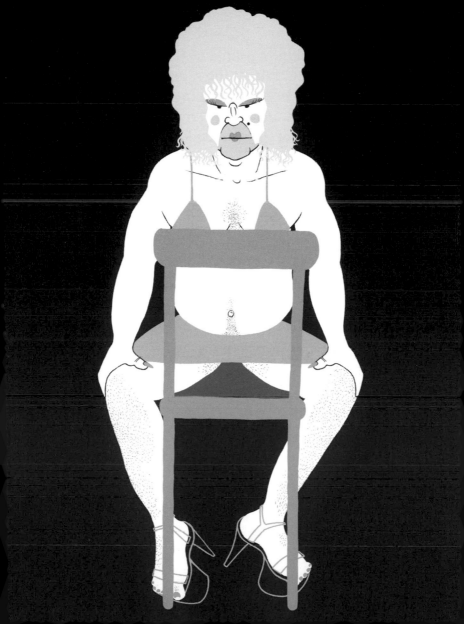

213 Drinking 12 pints of Guinness makes you irresistible to the ladies. It also makes you a better pool player, an invincible bare knuckle fighter, and increases the size of your cock.

214 You can lead a horse to water, but if you can get it to breakdance then you've really got something.

215

Few things in life will bring a feeling of pure joy as much as seeing a telly on a stand being wheeled into your classroom.

216

Publishers!
When laying out *Eat Well, Stay Fit, Die Anyway*, make sure you end the book with a really great rule. Not a shit one like this.

Thanks

Mr Holy Moly says

Massive thanks to The Missus, the 3 Amigos, all the other Beasts, all my Moles especially HM094 for sifting through the millions of rules every day and HM039 for his indefatigable spirit (you'll get laid soon, I'm sure), big 'shout out' to the tribe at HMPJ and Sabretooth Law for making sure I get to keep my house.

Thanks also to Neil Sean and Victoria Newton (you make waking up worthwhile – I love your uselessness more than life itself!).

Thanks to all the stupid celebrities around the world. Please don't get clever – I'd be out of a job.

Thanks also to everyone that submitted rules to the site – obviously I would never have had the inclination, patience or talent to write these things myself, so without you etc etc blah blah blah.

And finally – thanks to anyone that bought the first book and everyone that reads the mailout – hurray!

Ben says

Big thanks to Mr Holy Moly and The Friday Project for another opportunity to draw rude pictures for money and also to the lovely Jess for putting up with a boyfriend that spends far too much time hunched over a laptop, grumbling about deadlines.